D1362669

ROMANIA

souvenir

Photos: Florin Andreescu

Text: Mariana Pascaru

English version: Alistair Ian Blyth

Editor: Dana Ciolcă

©Ad Libri Publishing House, Edition 2019

All rights to the present work are reserved for Ad Libri publishing house and reproduction, whether in part or in whole, of the text or illustrations herein is allowed only with the prior written consent of Ad Libri.
phone/fax: 021-212.35.67, 210.88.64, 610.37.92; 0722.527.876
e-mail: adlibri@adlibri.ro
www.adlibri.ro
www.calator-pe-mapamond.ro

Descrierea CIP a Bibliotecii Naționale a României
Romania - Souvenir / foto: Florin Andreescu; text: Mariana Pascaru;
        București: Ad Libri, 2018
          ISBN 978-606-8050-89-8
I. Andreescu, Florin (foto)
II. Pascaru, Mariana (text)

ROMANIA
souvenir

Photos: Florin Andreescu
Text: Mariana Pascaru

Ad**Libri**

10 reasons to visit Romania

Romania is becoming a name more and more well known in the European landscape. More and more people are declaring themselves captivated by this vibrant and colourful land, which has not yet become a standardised tourist product. Romania is undoubtedly a place which has every chance of attracting the attention of those tourists who are in search of the authentic, as the phenomenon of globalisation has not yet taken hold here.

Ask one hundred people and each will give you a different reason as to why Romania is worth visiting… Each will have found what he or she is looking for. And in Romania there are indeed many things to discover.

In what follows, we shall list a few of these reasons and try to identify the features that define Romania. The result will be a portrait sketch which, we hope, will entice you to come here. Each of you will fill in this sketch your own impressions, the details and adventures with animate any journey.

1 Romania is the best place in which to explore the Europe that lies at "the gates of the Orient".

Let yourself be seduced by its blend of east and west, by the efficiency and dynamism characteristic of the west, and the carefree relaxation of the east! There are places here where you will feel the thrum and the pulse of the present, and others where you will feel as though you have been transported from the present back to the inaccessible past.

2 Romania is a country unique among the mainly Slavic nations of south-eastern Europe, a land where the language spoken is Latin in origin.

Many Romanian words will probably sound familiar to speakers of the Romance languages who come to this land that borders Bulgaria, Hungary, Serbia, Moldova and Ukraine. The Roman legions, under the Emperor Hadrian, crossed the Danube in 101 A.D., conquered the Dacians, and colonised the southern regions of Dacia. The archaeological remains of ancient *Dacia Felix* can still be seen today.

3 In Romania you will find a whole new world just waiting to be discovered.

The magic of the lie of its land and myriad natural curiosities, the blend of archaic, anachronistic, kitsch and modern, the picturesque customs that have survived in many places, and the spectacular cities with their eclectic architecture all make up a world of surprising diversity.
For those who don't care for the beaten track and prefer the unpredictable, making discoveries for themselves, Romania is the ideal choice.

4 It is in Romania that the Danube ends its journey. Before emptying into the Black Sea, the river forms a spectacular delta, which has been declared a Biosphere Reserve.

After rising in the Black Forest in Germany, the Danube crosses ten countries and four capitals (2,860 kilometres). Immediately after entering Romania, the Danube forms a wild gorge, between Bazias and Drobeta-Turnu Severin, whose most spectacular stretch is named the Cauldrons.

With a surface area of 4,178 km^2, the Danube Delta is, in terms of size, the twenty-second largest in the world and the third largest in Europe. It is home to the largest area of compact reed beds in the world. According to the RAMSAR Treaty, it is a Wetland of International Importance, and is listed as a UNESCO World Natural Heritage site.

5 Romania is like many worlds rolled into one, and this will give added flavour to your journey. Passing from one Romanian province to another will give you an opportunity to see many multicultural milieus, which have preserved traces of their turbulent history.

Romania is made up of provinces, the so-called mediaeval *ţări* (lands) – small voevoda princedoms and independent states ruled by *knjazija* (feudal overlords), each with its own distinctive character and history. In the twelfth century, King Géza II of Hungary sent Saxon colonists to the Romanian province of Transylvania, who founded fortified settlements (Sighişoara, Sibiu, Bistriţa). The province was later annexed by the Austro-Hungarian Empire. The province of Dobrudja, colonised by the Greeks in the seventh century B.C., was part of the Roman Empire and later ruled by the Turks, between 1417 and 1878. The princes of Moldova, a province with numerous ruined forts and princely palaces, were tireless in their fight against the invading Turks. It is said that St Stephen the Great built a church after each of his victories against the Mahommedans. Indeed, in Moldavia you will find numerous mediaeval churches, adorned with exterior murals of breathtaking beauty. In the eighteenth century, Wallachia and Moldavia were ruled by the Phanariots, Greeks from the Phanar district of Constantinople, who were appointed by the Ottoman Porte; this was a period in which the Romanian milieu became imbued with oriental manners. During the Russo-Turkish War of 1828-29, Russian troops, led by Pavel Kiseleff, occupied Moldavia and Wallachia, remaining until 1834.

6 Romania is a fascinating subject for political analysis. Two periods have been decisive in Romania's history: that of the monarchy, when the country set out on the road of modernisation, and that of the communist dictatorship, whose consequences were disastrous.

In 1859, under the rule of Alexandru Ioan Cuza, the United Principalities were formed (Moldavia and Wallachia), which became Romania in 1862. In 1866, Carol of Hohenzollern-Sigmaringen (Carol I) came to the throne of the United Principalities, and a democratic constitution, inspired by that of Belgium, was adopted. Following the Russo-Turkish War of 1877, Romania obtained complete independence and freedom from the Ottoman yoke, and in March 1881 it was proclaimed the Kingdom of Romania, with Carol I as the first King. The long and beneficial rule of Carol I (1866-1914) was followed by that of his descendents: Ferdinand I, Carol II, and Mihai I. On 1 December 1918, the Act of Union between Transylvania, the Banat, Maramureș, Crișana, and Romania was signed in Alba Iulia. The communists, who seized power after the Second World War, isolated Romania from the rest of Europe, exerting an extremely authoritarian rule and bequeathing Romania a harsh legacy. After more than forty years, the communist regime was toppled in 1989. Since 2007, Romania has been part of the European Union and is trying to rediscover the old values that were almost annihilated by the communists.

7 Romania is a land of religious belief. You will be impressed by the large number and variety of churches.

The ethnic diversity of Romania is reflected in its churches, which are built in the most various architectural styles. You will, of course, discover thousands of Orthodox places of worship – for this is a land which, although its language is Latin in origin, is part of Eastern Orthodox Christendom – as well as churches of the Evangelical denomination (the fortified churches of the Transylvanian Saxons), and the Hungarian, Szekler (Șumuleu), Polish (Cacica), and Armenian (Hagigadar) communities. You will also find Jewish synagogues (Timișoara) and Turkish mosques (Constanța, Mangalia).

8 The cities of Romania have much more to offer than you could ever imagine. Explore them and discover all their secrets! Many have preserved their historic centres, with enchanting winding streets, ideal for walks.

There are baroque cities, such as Timișoara; mediaeval citadels, such as Sighișoara; eclectic cities with frenetic boulevards, but also tranquil lanes, part of the old *mahalale* (tradesmen's quarters), such as the capital Bucharest; cities with tenement blocks that copy Soviet architecture, such as Bacău; cities that were formerly the capital of the land, with old princely courts, such as Tîrgoviște and Curtea de Argeș; cities with a definite tourist appeal, such as Brașov; but also declining industrial cities, with abandoned factories… The dynamic big cities have tempting cultural attractions. Sibiu was European Capital of Culture 2007, the prestigious Transylvania International Film Festival is held in Cluj annually, and Bucharest is host to the biannual George Enesco International Festival and Competition, to which are invited the most famous orchestras and conductors in the world.

9 Agricultural tourism is an ideal choice for a holiday in true Romanian style.

Romanian villages have discovered in recent years the rural development benefits of agricultural tourism. The rural communities of Bukowina, Maramureș, and the Rucăr-Bran corridor have blazed the trail. Old traditions and occupations can be admired in the fishing villages of the Danube Delta, the sheep-rearing villages of Mărginimea Sibiului, the coopers' villages of Bukowina (Pleșa, Bogata), and the potters' villages of Horezu, Vama and Marginea, which are like vast open-air pottery workshops. Rural folk wear traditional costume at Easter and Christmas, when *cozonac* and *pască* are baked, eggs are painted, and children go carolling from house to house.

In Bukowina, a village such as Ciocănești, with its stuccoed houses, will seem to you like something from a fairy tale. And in the Delta, a fishing village, Sfîntu Gheorghe – situated at the place where the Danube empties into the sea – fills with cinema-lovers from all over the world in the middle of August, when this isolated rural corner hosts the Anonimul International Independent Film Festival.

10 The local cooking, although not widely known, is full of flavour.

Try a few of the local traditional dishes, prepared according to age-old recipes, from fresh and healthy ingredients: pork-belly broth ("ciorbă"), stuffed cabbage leaves ("sărmăluțe") with cream and maize porridge ("mămăliguță"), cauldron chicken, skinless beef, pork and mutton mince sausages ("mititei"), Pleșcoi sausages, lamb pudding ("drob"), shepherd's maize porridge with cream and melted cheese ("bulz")… For dessert, try Brașov pies or curd pancakes ("papanași") with cream and jam. And to go with your meal, try a Romanian wine from the vineyards of Valea Călugărească, Tohani, Pietroasa, or Niculițel, ideally to be savoured to the accompaniment of lively Romanian folk music.

Romania is being talked about more and more, and more and more tourists are coming here to spend their holidays, in search of something different.
But don't forget that Romania is not just limited to one or other of the aspects presented above. Try to see as much as you can if you are coming for the first time. Discover Romania in the bustle of its cities, as well as in the tranquillity of its villages, seemingly frozen in past times, or on the Black Sea coast and the fantastic aquatic world of the Danube Delta, or on the heights of the Carpathians, with their hundreds of hiking trails and their spectacular lakes and gorges, where rare species of flora and fauna have been identified.
And, of course, look around you carefully and you will discover all the picturesque local peculiarities – after all, you have arrived at the gateway to the Balkans, where everything is more colourful than anywhere else!

Seemingly endless expanses of ploughed
fields extend around Romanian villages.

Country roads, Dobruja

Cart tracks lined with wild plants cut
across the fields.

At the edge of the plains of Dobrudja
wind turbines have begun to make
their appearance.

Ciocăneşti, a village turned into a museum
due to its decorated houses, a tradition that
was born in the 1950s

In the mountains settlements of scattered houses predominate: such is the case of Mătișești village in the Apuseni Mountains.

Rhododendrons, common in the high Carpathians, can also be found in the Ciucaș Mountains.

Edelweiss (*Leontopodium alpinum*), a protected species of plant, grows on the highest peaks of the Romanian mountains.

Flowering apple trees in an orchard in
Voineşti (Dîmboviţa). Known for its *Frumosul
de Voineşti* variety, every year the village hosts
an Apple Festival after the harvest.

Endless fields of sunflowers
stretching to the horizon –
one of the most moving vistas
of a journey through Romania

Following pages:
Along the southern Romanian coast, which
stretches between Cape Midia and Vama
Veche, you can encounter wild, rocky shores
as well as fine, sandy beaches.

The Danube Delta – a true aquatic paradise

Waiting for sunset, in the Delta

The Danube Delta is a labyrinth of channels,
swamps, lakes, sandbanks and endless
corridors of reeds.

The Danube Delta, a paradise for birds, is renowned for its numerous nesting colonies. In the Roșca-Buhaiova area, there can be found the largest colony of pelicans in Europe.

Expanses of water, reeds, and gnarled trees, draped in lianas, make up the miraculous world of the Delta.

Of the 320 species of birds identified in the Danube Delta, approximately 200 nest here, the rest being migratory. The most common birds are aquatic (140 species):
Pygmy cormorant - *Phalacrocorax pygmaeus*
Purple heron - *Ardea purpurea*
Grey heron - *Ardea cinerea*
Great egret - *Egretta alba*
Little egret - *Egretta garzetta*
Squacco heron - *Ardeola ralloides*
Common spoonbill - *Platalea leucorodia*
Glossy ibis - *Plegadis falcinellus*
Whooper swan - *Cygnus cygnus*
Common shelduck - *Tadorna tadorna*
(from left to right)

In the Delta, the air throbs to
myriad wing beats.
Here, you can see birds such as:
Ferruginous duck - *Aythya nyroca*
Steppe buzzard - *Buteo buteo vulpinus*
Peregrine falcon - *Falco peregrinus*
Avocet - *Recurvirostra avosetta*
Black-winged stilt - *Himantopus himantopus*
Common tern - *Sterna hirundo*
Eurasian kingfisher - *Alcedo athis athis*
European roller - *Coracias garrulus*
Eurasian hoopoe - *Upupa epops*
Penduline tit - *Remiz pendulinus*

35

Luxuriant, primordial vegetation covers
the expanses of water and earth between
the Delta's channels.

The old Sulina
Lighthouse, built by the
European Lower Danube
Commission in 1870

Following pages:
A colony of pelicans in the Danube Delta

After entering Romanian territory, the Danube forms a spectacular gorge, the most impressive section being the Cauldrons (9km).

◄

Babacai Rock, by the village of Coronini (formerly Pescari), in the Danube gorge

The impressive *Cross of Heroes*, 33 m in height, rises on the Șaua Mare platform of Mount Caraiman (2,291 m).

Gaura Valley in the Bucegi Mountains and Omu Chalet

▶

The Gutii Mountains, with
its Cockerel Crest, formed of
volcanic rocks

The volcanically formed Călimani Mountains, on whose plateau rise up the twelve Apostles Rocks

Following pages:
On a peninsula of the Bilea tarn, at 2,034m above sea level, there is an alpine cabin. Numerous trails set out from the area, toward the peaks and cabins of the Făgăraş Mountains.

Only a few thousand black goats (*Rupicapra rupicapra*) survived in the Romanian mountains, so this species is protected today by law.

Fortunately, the Carpathian Stag
(*Cervus elaphus*) is still a presence quite
common in the Romanian forests.

Although not as much as before, agriculture
and animal husbandry are still important
occupations in Maramureș.

Poienile Izei, a "rural paradise", hidden
among hills and mountains

With a surface area of more than 200,000 hectares
of vineyards, Romania is one of the most important
wine producers in Europe. Viticulture has a long
tradition in these lands.

Drăgăşani is an old wine growing and making centre. In the sixteenth century, these were the vineyards of the Buzescu, Ghica, Ştirbei and Bibescu boyar families, and even of Prince Matei Basarab.

Houses scattered over the hills of the
Rucăr-Bran Corridor

The geological and geomorphic reserve of Ripa Roșie, on the right slope of the Sebeș Valley

The end of the season of autumn labours

The matchless colours
of the Romanian forest

Following pages:
The sanctuary at Sarmizegetusa Regia
(Hunedoara county)

The road around Izvorul Muntelui
Lake (Bicaz) is 35km long and provides
breathtaking views.

Vidraru Reservoir, on the course of the Argeș River, next to the high-altitude Transfăgărășan national highway, which traverses, for 91.5km, the crests of the Făgăraș Mountains, at more than 2,000m above sea-level

As in olden days, peasants still
use horses and carts.

View towards Sadova, a charming village
that stretches between the Hills of Bucovina

Bucegi Mountains, as evening falls

Snow-covered limestone
crest in the Bucegi Massif

65

Peștera village, with the Bucegi
Mountains in the background

The scattered homesteads of Măgura
village, Rucăr-Bran corridor

Sheep wintering in the village

In a mountain village scattered among the hills, bringing in the hay is a real challenge.

Following pages:
The depths of winter in Șirnea, a village that lies at an altitude of 1,244m in the Piatra Craiului Mountains

The unaffected way in which children wear traditional costume is a striking feature of Romania.

The everyday life of young people in Romania does not seem different from that of their western counterparts. On festive days, however, they rediscover the picturesque beauty of their ancestral traditions.

Children from Oaș Country at
a folk celebration

Traditional still for "palinca", a kind of brandy
made from plums

Smithy in Botiza (Maramureș)

Reading from a book of hours

Sunday mass in Sadova, Bukowina

▶

Easter wouldn't be Easter without *pasca*. It takes patience and skill to bake it.

Father Berbecaru of Botiza Church, blessing the victuals (*pască*, *cozonaci*, painted eggs etc.) on Easter Day

▶

The wooden churches of Maramureș are impressive
for the consummate harmony of their proportions.
The church in Plopiș dates from the 17th century.

The Church of the Blessed Paraschiva in Desești preserves priceless murals.

Following pages:
First snows in Ieud, Maramureș

The blue pigment of the murals of Voroneţ
Monastery church, built by St Stephen the
Great in 1488, have long been famous.

Moldovița Monastery (1532), founded by Petru Rareș, one of the most famous painted churches of Bukowina

The church of the Humor Monastery is
one of the most impressive monuments
of Romanian mediaeval art.

Sucevița Monastery (late fourteenth
century), the most fortified monastic
complex in all Moldavia

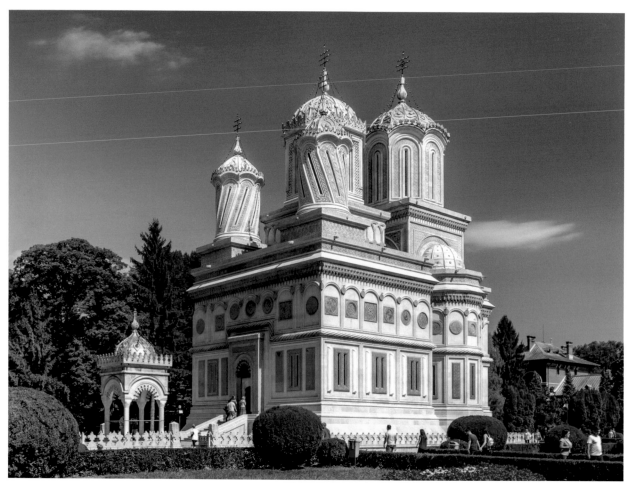

Curtea de Argeş, the former capital of the Romanian Land (14th-15th centuries), is famous for its beautiful Episcopal Church. Here can be found the tombs of the members of the former Romanian Royal Family.

◄

In the village of Romanii de Jos, three kilometres from Horezu (a traditional centre for pottery), can be found the most representative complex of Romanian mediaeval architecture in Wallachia, definitive of the Brâncoveanu style: the Hurezi Monastery (1690-1703).

At the centre of the rural settlements founded by Saxon colonists in the Romanian province of Transylvania in the twelfth century there stand fortified churches, which once served as places of refuge in times of danger.

The fortified church at Meșendorf, near Brașov

Seven of these churches have been
named UNESCO World Heritage sites.

The fortified church at Dirjiu

Following pages:
The fortified church at Saschiz

Biertan, in Sibiu County, is an important centre of the Saxon community.

Traditional Saxon costume

In Dobruja there used to be a large community of Tartars and Turks, who have left behind numerous mosques. The Carol I Mosque (1910-1912) is among the most beautiful.

◀

Coral Temple, the largest mosaic worship place in Bucharest

The Tînjaua on the Mara, an old agrarian
custom of Maramureș, which unfolds
every year in early May at Hoteni

On the feast of the Dormition of the
Theotokos (15 August), long processions
of children dressed in white and adults
bearing church flags set off on a
pilgrimage to Moisei Monastery.

Traditional wedding procession, Țara Oașului

In 2005, the Romanian tradition of the *Căluș* was declared by UNESCO to be a masterpiece of humanity's oral and non-material heritage. In former times, it was believed that the dance had healing powers, drove out evil spirits, and replenished the fertility of the land.

The Lole represent an old custom observed
by the Saxons from the villages along the
Hîrtibaci Valley (Sibiu). Groups of people
dressed in colourful rag costumes and wearing
scary masks dance through the village, making a hellish racket.

Before the Easter fast, in the village Brănești (20km from Bucharest), the "Kuč" festival is held, a rite that is Slavic in origin. Masked young men disguised as old crones, harlots or brides roam the village lanes and strike the people they meet with rods to protect them from evil and disease (the kuker in the photograph is from Păunești, Vrancea).

At Rișnov there is a stone fort built in the fourteenth century by the Teutonic Knights on a 150m-high crag. The fort offers breathtaking views of the Bîrsa Land.

Bran, an old customs point, for it was here that the main commercial road linking Transylvania (Brașov) and the Romanian Land (Cimpulung Muscel) passed, was defended by a stone fortress – Castle Bran.

The building in the Bavarian style next to
Castle Peleș, which housed the staff of the royal
court, has been converted into a hotel.

Peleș Castle, the summer residence of the royal family of Romania, built between 1875 and 1883 at the behest of Carol I of Hohenzollern-Sigmaringen

The historic centre of Sibiu, declared a reserve of mediaeval architecture, has wholly conserved its original features.

◀

The Council Tower, located between The Big Square and the Small Square, is part of the second chain of fortifications built around Sibiu between 1224 and 1241.

111

Sighişoara, a mediaeval citadel founded by Saxon colonists in 1191, preserves narrow, cobbled streets and vaulted passageways.

View of the Sighisoara Fortress from the "Lunca Poştei" Hill

▶

Mediaș, once one of the seven most important Transylvanian cities, preserves a part of its mediaeval walls.

Alba Iulia: the Roman-Catholic Cathedral of St Michael (thirteenth century), which houses the sarcophagus of Iancu of Hunedoara, and the Orthodox Cathedral of the Holy Trinity (1922), where King Ferdinand I of Romania was crowned

Baia Mare, in the foothills of the Gutii
Mountains, attested as a major mining centre
since 1329, was granted the right to build its
own defensive walls and bastions in 1469.

The Secession-style Palace of
the Prefecture and the Palace
of Culture in Tirgu-Mureș

Bistrița was founded by German colonists in
the 12th century. The symbol of Bistrița is the
Evangelical Church (15th-century), with its 74m
gothic tower, later altered in the Renaissance style.

Oradea, the largest city in Crișana, is known for its numerous Art Nouveau buildings, which date from the early twentieth century

Seemingly a patriarchal provincial city with
little over 300,000 inhabitants, Cluj-Napoca
harbors a strong and performing economy,
based on IT services.

First marked in ofcial documents over 700 years ago, Brașov is the most important citadel founded by the Saxon colonists in Transylvania.

Following pages:
Union Square in Timișoara has largely preserved its eighteenth-century baroque character.

The plateau in the centre of Piatra Neamț,
home to the old Princely Court, of which the
Church of St John the Baptist (1497-8) and
the Tower of Stephen the Great (1499) have
been preserved

The neo-Gothic Palace of Culture in Jassy, built between 1907 and 1926 on the site of the former princely court, designed by architect I.D. Berindey, is now a vast museum complex.

The cliff port of Constanța is dominated by
the elegant silhouette of the Casino, built
between 1907-1910, in the Art Nouveau
style.

The Art Museum in Craiova, housed in the Jean Mihail Palace, built between 1898 and 1907 by architect Paul Gottereau

Following communist "systematisation", an entire district of old houses in the centre of Bucharest was levelled to make way for the gigantic House of the People (now the Palace of Parliament) and the Union Boulevard.

The Palace of Justice, situated on the bank of the Dîmboviţa River is representative of the French neo-Renaissance style that influenced the architecture of Bucharest in the 19th and 20th centuries.

Stavropoleos Church (1724) in Bucharest,
one of the most beautiful examples of the
late Brîncoveanu style

The Patriarchate (seventeenth century) dominates the hill that overlooks Union Square in central Bucharest.

Following pages:
Calea Victoriei is the most elegant thoroughfare of the capital and is flanked by superb buildings, such as the former Royal Palace (today the National Art Museum of Romania).

The Romanian Athenaeum, built between 1886
and 1888 in the neoclassical style by Albert
Galleron, is crowned by a baroque cupola.

An annex behind the magnificent Art Nouveau Cantacuzino palace houses a museum dedicated to Romania's most famous composer, Georges Enesco, who lived there for a short period.

The Museum of the Village is a blessed oasis of peace in the midst of a crowded capital.

Herăstrău Park, on the banks of Herăstrău Lake (70 hectares), in the north of the city, is the largest park in Bucharest (187 hectares).

▶

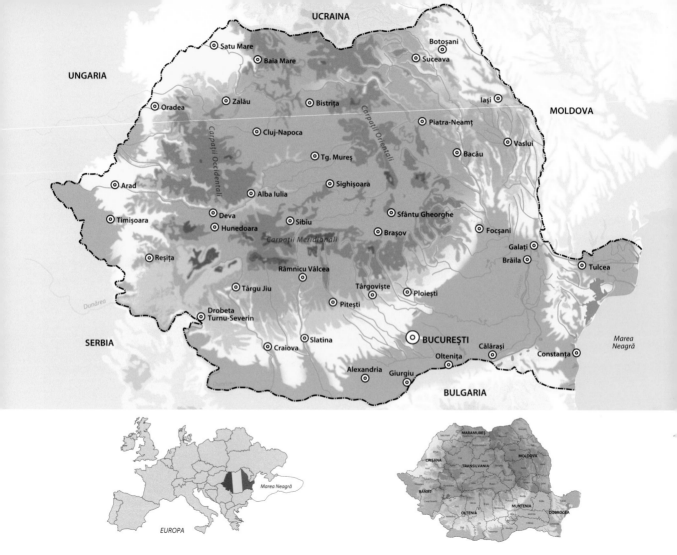

Romania

General information

Official language: Romanian

Location: Romania is located in southeastern Europe and borders Ukraine (in the north and east), Moldova (in the east), Hungary (in the west and northwest), Serbia (in the southwest) and Bulgaria (in the south).

Surface area: 238,391km²

Government: Bicameral parliamentary republic

European Status: member of the European Union since 1 January 2007.

Flag: Blue, yellow and red in vertical stripes, from left to right, respectively

Population: 20,121,641 people (2011), of which 89% are Romanian. The principal minorities include Hungarians and Szeklers (Secui) (6.5%) and Roma (Gypsies) (3.3%)

Religions: Christian-Orthodox (86.8%), Protestant (3.5%), Catholic (5%), Graeco-Catholic (Uniate) (1%)

Capital: Bucharest (2,064,000 inhabitants), first mentioned in 1459. Approx. 2,000,000 people.

Important cities: Timişoara, Iaşi, Constanţa, Braşov, Cluj-Napoca, Oradea

Time zone: GMT +3 hours in summertime (from the last Sunday of March to the last Sunday of October), and GMT +2 hours for the rest of the year.

Climate: Temperate continental. The average summer temperature is between 22° and 24°C, although maximum temperatures can reach 38°C. In winter the average temperature is typically below -3°C.

National currency: LEU. 1 Leu = 100 Bani. Currently circulating banknotes: 1, 5, 10, 50, 100, 200 and 500 Lei. Currently circulating coins: 1, 5, 10 and 50 Bani.

Official Public Holidays: December 1st – Romanian National Day, January 1st and 2nd – New Year, May 1st – Labour Day, first and second day of Easter, December 25th and 26th – Christmas.

The natural setting

Although Romania has a surface area of just under 240,000 square kilometres, it can boast almost all forms of geographical relief: mountains, sea, delta, lakes, hills, winding valleys, caves, gorges, waterfalls...

For 1,075 kilometres through Romania, the Danubius, the sacred river of the Dacians, offers magnificent vistas. In the Banat, along the banks of the Danube, sub-Mediterranean vegetation flourishes (in spite of the fact that we find ourselves in a zone of continental climactic influence) and mysterious karst formations can be found. The Cauldrons sector of the Danube Gorges is the most spectacular: in former times, this section of the river resembled the boiling, churning water in a fisherman's cauldron, whence the name.

Before it empties into the Black Sea, the Danube splits into three long branches (Chilia, Sulina and Saint George), between which a wild delta has formed. At not more than ten thousand years old, this is the youngest terrain in the country. A "paradise" for all kinds of plants and wild animals, the Danube Delta has been declared a UNESCO world biosphere reservation.

More than half the length of the Carpathian Mountains, which are part of the Alpine-Carpathian-Himalayan chain, is to be found within the territory of Romania. There is snow cover in the mountains for between one hundred and one hundred and twenty days a year. In the mountains, there are numerous marked hiking routes, with varying degrees of difficulty. The most accessible mountain resorts are in the Prahova Valley, which is flanked by the Bucegi and Baiului Mountains: Sinaia, the former summer residence of the royal family, Bușteni, Azuga, Predeal. The Făgăraș Massif holds the record for altitude, with its almost unassailable Moldoveanu peak (2,544m). Piatra Craiului is a crest of grey-white limestone, with precipices, rocky shelves, crags and scree. The Retezat Massif, with its eighty glacial tarns (Bucura, Zănoaga, Black Tarn, Ana, Lia, Viorica), is home to a national park of 54,400 hectares, and has been declared a Biosphere Reservation. The Maramureș Mountains are traversed by the Vaser Valley, along the length of which runs an old-fashioned narrow-gauge steam railway. In Guții, one is particularly struck by the Cockerel Crest – a sheer wall of volcanic rock with an altitude of 1,438 metres. The Rodnei Mountains preserve numerous glacial traces: crests, valleys, morains. We cannot speak of the Rarău Massif without mentioning the mysterious Lady's Rocks. On the plateau of the Călimani Mountains, which are of volcanic origin, there tower the Twelve Apostles Rocks, which seem to transport us to the mythic beginnings of the world.

The Carpathian Mountains have been called a "stronghold of waters". For it is here that hundreds of rivers and streams begin their journey through Romania, representing ninety-eight per cent of the country's hydrographic network: the Olt, Mureș, Ialomița, Someș, Argeș, Siret, Jiu, Criș. The course of these waters through the mountains of Romania often offers magnificent spectacles. The Nerei, Turzii, Bistrița, Oltețului, Runcului, Bicazului, and Tătarului are just some of the country's two hundred gorges.

Beneath Romania lie hidden around twelve thousand caves, whose galleries stretch for one thousand kilometres: the Scărișoara Glacier, the Cave of Bears, Bistrița Cave, the Cave of the Women, the Cave of the Bats, Ialomița Cave, the Cave of Wind, Meziad Cave. Romania can boast some three thousand five hundred lakes. There are volcanic lakes (St Ana), glacial lakes (Bucura, Zănoaga, Gîlcescu, Bîlea), karst lakes (Iezerul Ighiu), saline lakes (Bottomless Lake, Ursu Lake), natural dams (Red Lake), man-made reservoirs (the Iron Gates, on the Danube, Izvorul Muntelui or Bicaz, on the Bistrița, Vidraru, on the Argeș, Vidra, on the Lotru, and Scropoasa, on the Ialomița).

Unesco World Cultural and Natural Heritage sites

The nucleus of the Dacian kingdom – **the Dacian Fortresses** – was to be found in the **Orăștiei Mountains** in the south west of Transylvania. Numerous forts, strategic structures and observation towers were spread over two hundred square kilometres in these mountains. The Dacian fortresses, built in the 1st century BC and the 1st century AD, conquered by the Romans in the early 2nd century AD, are among the most celebrated vestiges of these legendary ancestors of the Romanians, who considered themselves "immortals". These fortresses, enclosed by perfectly fitting walls of polished limestone blocks (*murus dacicus*), represent a "defensive system unique in European architecture". The military, political, economic and religious centre of the Dacians was Sarmizegetusa Regia. It is situated 1,200 metres above sea level, at the highest point of Grădiştea Hill. Many manmade terraces were carved out of the hillside. The upper plateau is connected to the sacred area of the sanctuaries on two terraces by a *via sacra* – a monumental paved road with limestone flags. Before it was conquered and destroyed by the Romans, Sarmizegetusa Regia was the most important metallurgical centre anywhere in Europe outside the Roman Empire.

The fortified churches of Transylvania, which look like small citadels, were built in particular after the Tartar invasion of 1241. There are approximately one hundred and fifty villages which preserve such monuments. Seven of these churches have been named UNESCO world heritage sites: Biertan, Cîlnic, Dîrjiu, Prejmer, Saschiz, Valea Viilor and Viscri.

Sighişoara, one of the few inhabited citadels in the world, is a beautiful illustration of mediaeval city building. The Sighişoara citadel, built in 1191 by Saxon colonists on a hill overlooking the left bank of the Tîrnava Mare River, has preserved precisely the elements of the mediaeval universe.

Nowhere in Romania can more churches, monasteries, and hermitages be found in such a compact area as in **Bukowina**. Most of them are hundreds of years old. The exterior walls of a number of churches in Bucovina are covered in murals painted in incomparable hues of red, yellow, blue and green. The church of Voroneţ Monastery is reckoned to be the "Sistine Chapel of the East". On the west facade of the church founded by Stephen the Great in 1488, there is a depiction of the Last Judgement. It was painted after 1547 against a background whose inimitable shade of blue has long become famous... The origin of the "Voroneț blue" have still not been elucidated.

In Wallachia, in the village of Romanii de Jos, three kilometres from Horezu (a traditional centre for pottery), can be found the most representative complex of Romanian mediaeval architecture, definitive of the Brîncoveanu style: **Hurez Monastery** (1690-1703). During the time of Constantin Brîncoveanu (1688-1714), Hurez Monastery was a major and thriving centre of culture and the arts: here there was an extensive library (with four thousand volumes), unique in south-east Europe at the beginning of the 18th century, a school for copyists, scribes and grammarians, and a school for painters, whose pupils then worked in Wallachia, Transylvania and south of the Danube.

Maramureș, a region in northern Romania, is renowned for its marvellous culture of woodworking, which has flourished in the villages along the Mara, Iza, Cosău, Vișeu and Tisa valleys. The portals of the locals, which are scrupulously carved with decorative motifs representing stylised solar disks, the tree of life, crosses, geometric figures, are remarkable examples of rustic art. Expressions of local spirituality, the wooden churches in the Maramureș villages of Bîrsana, Budești, Desești, Ieud, Plopiș, Poienile Izei, Rogoz and Surdești, with their tapering spires soaring to the heavens, seem to have overcome the perishable nature of the material from which they have been crafted.

The Danube Delta is one of the world's most extensive wetlands (2,681 square kilometres) and has the largest area of compact reed-beds. In this exotic delta, which lies between the Chilia, Sulina and Saint George branches of the Danube, more than 1,200 species of plants and trees, 300 species of birds and 100 species of fish have been identified. Approximately fifty per cent of the surface area of the Danube Delta is temporarily under water (particularly in spring), forty-five per cent is permanently under water, and just five per cent (spits of dry land) is never submerged.